THE MASS
IN PICTURES

A REDEMPTORIST PUBLICATION

THE MASS IN PICTURES

Text: John Trenchard, C.SS.R.
Christopher Gaffney, C.SS.R.

Photography: Charles Wooding, Dip.A.D.,
M.A. (Photography)
Front Cover: Michael Henesy, C.SS.R.

Design: Patrick Burton
Roger Smith

Drawings: Christopher Higham

The editors gratefully acknowledge the
assistance of Fr. Bernard Crowe, C.SS.R. and
the parishioners of Bishop's Stortford,
England in the preparation of this publication.

Nihil Obstat: G. Raimundus Can. Lawrence
                     Censor Deputatus
Imprimatur: + Antonius Emery
                     Episcopus Portus Magni
Portus Magni, die 19 iulii 1978

ISBN O 85231 043 9

© Redemptorist Publications 1978

Printed in Britain by
Knight & Forster Ltd.,
Water Lane, Leeds LS11 9UB

Contents

**My flesh is real food
and my blood is real drink.
He who eats my flesh
and drinks my blood
lives in me
and I live in him.**

The Mass in Pictures examines each part of the Mass in order. Over eighty photographs combine with the text to explain the meaning of the different parts of the Mass, to look into their background and history, and to lead people to a deeper understanding of the Mass and to a more effective sharing in it.

In presenting the Mass in this way *The Mass in Pictures* draws on history and tradition as well as reflecting the Church's latest thinking on the great Mystery of Faith.

On the same night that he was betrayed, the Lord Jesus took some bread, and thanked God for it and broke it, and he said, "This is my body, which is for you; do this as a memorial of me". In the same way he took the cup after supper, and said, "This cup is the new covenant in my blood. Whenever you drink it, do this as a memorial of me." (*I. Cor. II: 24-26*)

FROM THE EARLIEST DAYS, THE Christian community has come together to celebrate the Eucharist, or as we now refer to it, the Mass. The Acts of the Apostles, written around the year 70 A.D., tells how the early Christians met regularly for "the teaching of the apostles and the breaking of bread" (*Acts 2:42*). And in one of the most valuable documents we possess Justin the Martyr gives us this unique picture of the celebration of Mass in A.D. 150:

"On the day which is called Sun-Day, all, whether they live in the town or the country, gather in the same place.

Then the memoirs of the Apostles or the Writings of the Prophets are read for as long as time allows.

When the reader has finished, the president speaks, exhorting us to live by these noble teachings.

Then we rise all together and pray.

Then, as we said earlier, when the prayer is finished, bread, wine and water are brought. The president then prays and gives thanks as well as he can. And all the people reply with the acclamation: Amen!

Then the eucharistic gifts are distributed and shared out to everyone, and the deacons are sent to take them to those who are absent."

The Mass is a mystery which touches the life of the whole world. It is like an irresistible magnet which in the huge sprawling cities and the remotest villages stirs people out of their homes and groups them together around the Lord. The language can be different; the external shape and form can change; but the essence of the mystery remains always intact. Nothing has changed since Justin's day.

In this book we are going to enter more deeply into this most precious mystery. We will examine the different parts of the Mass and look carefully into their background and history. We hope that you will enjoy this prayerful reflection on the history, tradition, and the Church's latest thinking on the Mass. But more than anything, we hope this series will deepen our participation in this great Mystery of our Faith.

1. Preparing for Mass

It is God's People.

WHEN WE PASS THROUGH THE door of a church the world and its problems remain with us. The arthritis of the elderly man who has struggled through rain and wind, the screaming of the small child in the arms of her harrassed and embarrassed mother which has given the family a bad night and now seems destined to last throughout Mass do not miraculously disappear. Nor does the loneliness of the widower whose wife died ten years ago; nor the teenager's memory of the blazing row with her parents over a hurried breakfast half an hour previously. The congregation which gathers for Sunday Mass is always a strange group of people, with all the problems of the world.

Through the church door

It is also God's People. Sometimes we may think that our fellow-parishioners are not quite the kind of people we would choose. But they are the kind of people God chooses. Through the church door passes a cross-section of mankind. And in that congregation God brings mankind to himself.

At home

When we enter someone's home we knock to be let in. When we enter the church there is no question of first knocking on the door. It is our home; where we belong. Only when we make ourselves "at home" can God deepen our union with him and with one another.

A moment in prayer

As we enter the church, then, we make the sign of the cross, which reminds us of the life of the Trinity which is ours and of those sufferings which we share with Christ. We should also spend a few minutes in quiet prayer before Mass starts to prepare ourselves for the peace which Christ offers us. When the congregation has assembled, united in suffering and in prayer, the Mass can begin.

The sign of the cross reminds us of the life of the Trinity which is ours.

A few minutes in quiet prayer before Mass starts.

2. Entrance

As the priest approaches the altar the whole congregation chant a psalm or hymn.

The kiss of greeting unites the priest with Jesus Christ and the saints in heaven.

THE ALTAR IS THE CENTRE OF THE Church. The Christian family gathers around it to celebrate the Eucharist. In the altar are contained some relics of saints and into the stone are cut five crosses, recalling our Lord's five wounds.

The approach

And so it is natural that the approach to the altar, a symbol of Christ himself and of the whole Church, should be a solemn one. As the priest approaches the altar the whole congregation open the Mass by chanting a psalm or hymn. This approach is important, for it sets the tone, the atmosphere, for the whole celebration. Indeed, the Syrians call the Mass simply *Kurobho* which means, "approach".

The greeting

Then, in a few brief words and actions, the scene is set. On reaching the altar the priest touches it with his lips. The altar represents Christ, the cornerstone, the foundation of the Church. It contains the bones of the saints. And so this kiss of greeting unites the priest with Jesus Christ and the saints in heaven. Together, priest and people make the sign of the cross, recalling the Trinity in whose name they celebrate the Mass. And in the name of the Father, Son and Holy Spirit, the priest greets the congregation, proclaiming the presence of the Lord to the assembled community.

The whole Church

These opening moments bring home to us that it is not merely one priest and a few parishioners who gather around the altar for the celebration of Mass. It is the whole Church. The Church on earth is united with Christ and the Church in heaven to give praise and glory to God our Father.

Together, priest and people make the sign of the cross.

The priest greets the congregation, proclaiming the presence of the Lord.

9

3.Penitential Rite

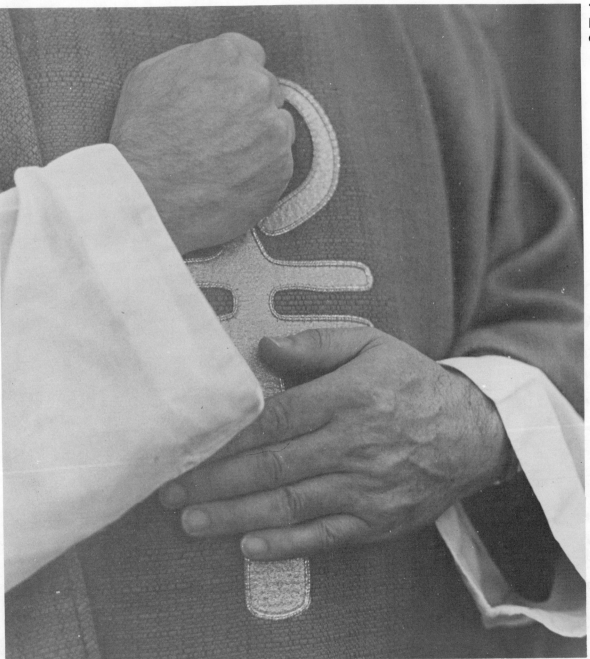

The priest strikes his breast during the "I confess".

ANY TALK OF PARTIES IN HEAVEN sounds very naive and childish. But why not ? After all, on the one occasion Jesus gave us a little peep into the life of heaven it was to show us the rejoicing that goes on when a sinner is forgiven.

Unfortunately, the enthusiastic joy of our friends in heaven hardly ever seems to spill over onto earth. Quite the reverse. Any mention of sin, even the forgiveness of sin, seems to plunge us into the doldrums.

The example of Christ

And that's a great pity, because our Lord set quite a different example. He sat down quite happily to celebration banquets with men like Zacchaeus and Matthew. As Fr Louis Evely reminds us : "Christ gaily invited himself to the table of sinners before inviting them ,in his turn, to his table of Communion."

And this is exactly what happens in that part of the Mass we call the "Penitential Rite". We are sinners, but Jesus Christ quite happily invites himself into our company. Naturally the priest is concerned that everyone's attention should be directed to the most important of all guests so he invites us to pause for a moment so that we are able, as it were, to pick out the Lord in the crowd.

Sitting down with the Lord

And it is important to find him. A lot of our boredom at Mass and with religion in general stems from the fact that we hardly ever look around us and notice the marvels of God. We still think religion is what we do for God and so we find the admission of our guilt rather depressing.

But this should not be. The priest

The rite of blessing and sprinkling holy water may replace the Penitential Rite. This reminds us of our baptism when our sins were forgiven.

strikes his breast during the "I confess" and reminds us that Christ's forgiveness is available to us. The Penitential Rite tells us of God's forgiveness.

O happy faults ! They remind us of the Father's loving tenderness and we feel the urge now to celebrate at the table of the Lord.

4.Gloria

Lóri-a in excélsis Dé-o.

BREAKING INTO SONG IS THE most natural thing in the world: except, it seems, at Mass. In many parish churches, neither the stick of a conductor nor the nudge of the organ can rouse the members of the congregation to open their mouths and sing.

The angels broke into song when Jesus Christ was born. The first Christians took up their joyful hymn. And at Mass, as Christ comes among us once again, we make the song of the angels our own: Glory to God in the highest, and peace to his people on earth.

A popular song

The *Gloria* takes us back to the very beginnings of our Faith. It began as a popular song which the people loved to sing. When they came together the first Christians would begin to sing their praises of God as naturally as we used to gather around the piano for a family get-together or as we sing our favourite tune in the bath. And so it is not surprising that the simple melody of the *Gloria* soon found its way into the celebration of the Eucharist. By the year 530 it had become an accepted part of the feastday Mass.

A sign of love

"To sing belongs to lovers" wrote St Augustine. We express and deepen our love for someone in song. In the *General Instruction of the Roman Missal* the Church emphasises that "singing should be widely used at Mass" to show our love for God: and reminds us of the ancient proverb that "He prays twice who sings well'.

Brings the Mass to life

Singing helps to bring the Mass to life. The *Gloria,* as are all the prayers of the Mass, is ancient, but not antiquated. It is a prayer to be sung from the heart, not a legal formula to be read.

"Let the punishment fit the crime" is a familiar legal formula that we can imagine being whispered in the darkened corridors of Justice. But listen to the Mikado singing it:

"My object all sublime
I shall achieve in time —
To let the punishment fit the crime —
The punishment fit the crime."

Quite a difference, isn't there?

"You alone ..."

In the Penitential Rite we confessed our sin in the presence of Christ. Now, it is the most supernatural thing in the world to rejoice and glory in that presence. We can only open our mouths and hearts, and sing:

"You alone are the Holy One,
you alone are the Lord,
you alone are the Most High,
Jesus Christ,
with the Holy Spirit,
in the glory of God the Father.
  Amen."

He prays twice who sings well.

13

5.Collect

WHEN WE ARRIVE AT OUR PLACE of work, whether it be factory, building-site, school or office, we pause for a moment, perhaps exchanging a few words with our friends or snatching a quick glance at the paper; or simply gazing into space wishing that last night had not been quite so riotous. The pause may last only a minute or two. But it is important. It breaks the morning frantic rush and adjusts us for the day of work ahead.

The *Opening Prayer* or *Collect* gives us a similar pause in the Mass. It forces us to stop and think and pray. It concludes the Introductory Rites and prepares us for the main part of the celebration which is about to begin.

Let us pray. The call to attention, like the cry of the sergeant-major, encourages those who were beginning to flag to stand erect: to concentrate. The silence that follows is a solemn one. Every one of us makes our own prayer, not in complicated words but in simply standing quietly in the presence of God. God alone knows what prayer is in the heart of each person at that moment.

Our prayer collected

But then follows a very different kind of prayer. The priest gathers or *collects* our silent prayers and presents them to God. The *Collect* is a "prayer of soberness and sense": the words are always concise, presenting the theme of the day and summarising the prayer of the whole community. Because it is a prayer of few words it demands our fullest attention: or we will suddenly discover that the prayer has finished before we had even started to listen.

While praying the *Collect* the priest extends his hands, as did Christ on the

The priest's prayer embraces all the Church's needs . . . it "collects" our silent prayers and presents them to God.

cross. This reminds us of two things. The priest's prayer is on behalf of everyone assembled and of the whole Church: it embraces all her needs. And the priest prays as Christ himself prays. Like Christ, he prays to the Father in the Holy Spirit.

Prayer like Christ's

Already in the Mass we have prayed several times in the name of the Blessed Trinity, Father, Son and Holy Spirit. The mystery of the Trinity is the central Mystery of our Faith. And the Mass, more than anything else draws us deeper into that Mystery. We will be saying much more about this. For the moment, let us remember that in the Mass most of our prayer is to God our Father. And in praying to the Father our prayer becomes like Christ's.

The silence is a solemn one.

6.Scripture Readings

It is as if the Lord is now saying to us: "I have a proposition to make and want to know what you intend to do about it."

THERE ARE SOME MOMENTS IN the Mass when Christ seems to be saying to us: "Please repeat this after me." The Opening Prayer is just one such occasion. When the priest says "Let us pray" we are invited in the brief silence that follows to try as best we can to ensure that our own thoughts coincide with the sentiments of the prayer.

When we come, however, to that part of the Mass where the Word of God is read, it is very different. Here we are expected to listen rather than speak. It is as if the Lord is now saying to us: "I have a proposition to make and want to know what you intend to do about it."

Three Readings

In the early days of the Church, the number and length of the readings was not fixed. Justin the Martyr, writing in A.D.150, tells us that the reader simply continued for as long as the time allowed. Nowadays, however, we are invited on Sundays to listen to three carefully prepared readings which are always in the following order: the Old Testament (replaced by the Acts of the Apostles in Paschal time), the writings of the Apostles, and, finally, the Gospel.

Inspired by God

St Paul writing to his friend Timothy reminded him that "all Scripture is inspired by God and can profitably be used for teaching, refuting error, for guiding peoples lives and teaching them to be holy." (*2 Tim. 3: 15-16*). The living word of God, in short, has the power to change us.

The power of man's word

We know from experience that the spoken word is very powerful indeed. Words can bring us happiness or extreme dejection. Try for a moment to recall just one occasion in your life when you perhaps overheard someone criticise you or were on the receiving end of a verbal lashing. The effect was probably devastating and it is an experience we all dread. On the other hand, just one word of encouragement or praise is all most of us need to face and overcome any amount of hardship in our lives.

The Jews believed that a word was far more than just a sound emitted by the mouth. "The spoken word to the Hebrew," writes Professor John Paterson, "was fearfully alive ... It was a unit of energy charged with power." To the Jew a word was so alive that it actually did things. Now just think again about those critical words that were aimed in your direction and you will begin to understand the Jewish mind. Were they not like bullets which slowly wormed their way into you and really upset you?

The power of God's word

When we remember this Jewish idea that words can actually do things, a new way of looking at the Bible opens up before us. We begin to see the Bible as a conversation between the Father and man. It is God who begins the conversation and at his word creation springs into being. "God said, 'Let there be light', and there was light ... God said, 'Let us make man in our own image, in the likeness of ourselves' ... and so it was."

Perhaps we can see now what we mean when we say that God's word is *creative*. And every page of the Bible adds to the splendour of this teaching by reminding us that God is Love. His words are the very opposite to those bullet-type words which gradually destroy man. They are words of love in which he gives himself, shares his secrets, and reveals himself to those who listen.

Listening

What, then, should our attitude be during the Liturgy of the Word? We can sum it up by saying it should be one of *listening* to and *responding* to what God has to say to us in the Readings. And that is why the psalm which is sung or said after the first reading is so important. We call it the Responsorial Psalm because it is one way of responding to the Word of God.

Speaking to Christians in the fourth century, Saint John Chrysostom gave them this advice we could well follow. "Do not sing the refrain out of routine. When you have listened to the reading, your voice should proclaim that you love Him above everything, that you prefer nothing to Him, that you burn with love for Him."

"When you have listened to the reading, your voice should proclaim that you love Him above everything . . . that you burn with love for Him."

7. Gospel

ONE SIMPLE BELIEF BRINGS US out of our homes each week to share with the whole parish in the mystery of the Mass: the belief that almost two thousand years ago God became man.

The prophets had dreamed of his coming. And when we listen carefully to the reading of the Old Testament at Mass, it is almost impossible not to share their dream and feel something of the intense longing of countless generations for the coming of the Saviour.

As the Book of the Gospels, the Word of God, is carried in procession we all join in an enthusiastic 'Alleluia!'

His word can enlighten our minds, strengthen our lips with the words of faith, and fill our hearts with the love of God.

It was a joyful night indeed when Jesus our Saviour was born. Scripture tells us that the angels greeted the first cries of the newborn baby with jubilant singing. And it was to be the same later when the divine child grew into a man and Jesus walked the dusty roads of Palestine. Those who heard him preach, teach, and felt his healing power, could hardly restrain themselves from literally singing his praises. "Hosanna", they sang, "to the Son of David!"

Alleluia!

It is not surprising, then, to find that there is an ancient tradition in the Church of joining together in joyful song as we prepare to listen to Jesus speaking to us in the Gospel. As the Book of the Gospels, the Word of God, is carried in procession, we are all encouraged to join in an enthusiastic Alleluia! It is a Hebrew cry of joy which is known the world over and in the setting of the liturgy means "Praise the Lord present in his Word".

Jesus speaks

For this is our belief. Jesus speaks to us when the Gospel is proclaimed. And so, following an ancient practice, the priest makes a sign of the cross over the first words of the sacred text before signing himself on the forehead, lips and breast. It is as though he were taking from Christ (represented by the Gospel) the grace of light and strength he offers to all.

And here is an important lesson we must not forget. We can take strength from the Word of God. Jesus will ask each one of us to do many things in his Gospel. But he will not leave us alone in our weakness. His word can enlighten our minds, strengthen our lips with the words of faith, and fill our hearts with the love of God.

The priest makes a sign of the cross over the first words of the sacred text before signing himself on the forehead, lips and breast. It is as though he were taking from Christ the grace of light and strength he offers to all.

WHEN A CHURCH IS CONSECRATED the bishop anoints the walls, in twelve different places, with the oil of chrism. Each place anointed in this way is marked with a cross and a candle-holder is placed beneath each cross. The consecration sets the seal on the church so that it can never afterwards be put to some profane use. The church-building is a sign of the Church: with "the apostles for its foundations, Jesus himself for its cornerstone", and built up by charity.

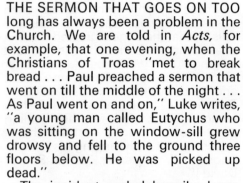

THE SERMON THAT GOES ON TOO long has always been a problem in the Church. We are told in *Acts,* for example, that one evening, when the Christians of Troas "met to break bread . . . Paul preached a sermon that went on till the middle of the night . . . As Paul went on and on," Luke writes, "a young man called Eutychus who was sitting on the window-sill grew drowsy and fell to the ground three floors below. He was picked up dead."

The incident ended happily, however. Paul brought the boy back to life. And then they "went back upstairs where he broke bread and carried on talking till daybreak."

Preaching the Gospel

Luke's bare outline of the story fails to reveal what Paul's over long sermon was about. But we can easily guess. Paul told his converts about the life and teachings of Jesus Christ. He preached the Gospel to them.

In the homily the priest continues to bring the Gospel to life. The words of Jesus are dead words as long as they remain stuck in a book. They only become living words when they are heard and accepted by us as words of eternal life. The priest's duty — indeed his primary duty — is to build up the faith of each one of us and of the whole Church by proclaiming the Gospel of God.

The embrace indicates the priest's desire to grasp the sacred word of God, which he then communicates to others in the homily.

It would be a mistake, then, to think of the homily as an instruction or a lecture. Rather, it continues the call of the Gospel. The priest takes the word of God that we have just heard and applies it to the concrete circumstances of life and to the particular needs of the congregation.

God's sacred word

This is symbolised by the priest kissing the Book of Gospels, at the same time praying: *"May the words of the Gospel wipe away our sins."* The embrace indicates the priest's desire to grasp the sacred word of God, which he then communicates to others in the homily. At times in the past the homily has been neglected, but today the Church recognises it as a part of the liturgy which "should not be omitted except for a serious reason."

The power to give life

The spaciousness of our local parish church may be very different from the intimacy of the hot and stuffy room in Troas. It is totally unlike the open Palestinian countryside walked by Jesus. But the message of the Gospel is unchanged. It is a message which will send to sleep those who do not want to hear it. To those, however, who listen with open ears it has the power to save; it has the power to bring back to life.

In the homily the priest brings the Gospel to life. He builds up the faith of each one of us and of the whole Church by proclaiming the Gospel of God.

9.Creed

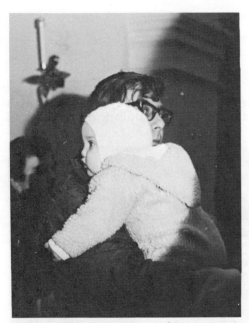

The Creed is the prayer of our baptism...

ON SUNDAYS AND CERTAIN FEAST days the whole congregation stands after the homily to pray the Creed together. And we use that word *pray* to set purpose. For many of us, even though we have recited or sung the Creed hundreds of times, never think of it as a prayer. We tend to regard it purely as a declaration of what we believe. But it is this and something more. It is, as Louis Evely puts it, "the prayer of our baptism, our confirmation, and our dying moments."

A little anecdote may help us to understand just what Father Evely means. It is about a little old lady who went to hear a very complicated lecture on God. "I did not understand much of it," she told her friend afterwards, "but I do know that he made God sound very great." That is exactly

The Creed speaks only of God and not at all of ourselves.

The Creed is a prayer which unites everyone in the Church.

"Let the Creed resound so that the true faith may be declared in sound, and that the souls of believers . . . may be ready to partake, in communion, of the Body and Blood of Christ."

what the Creed does. It makes God sound very great and leaves us in no doubt that in our living and our dying we are intimately bound up with the Father, Son and Holy Spirit.

Looks at God

That is why the Creed is one of our most treasured prayers. It speaks only of God and not at all of ourselves. In other words, it is a genuine prayer because it gets us "out of ourselves" and focuses all our attention on the Creator. When we recite the Creed at Mass, we are invited to take a close look at what God does and what he is. Now when we really do that, our whole inclination is to give him thanks and praise. And thanking and praising the Father through Christ our Lord is

what the Eucharist and the Mass is all about.

Origins

The Creed we now use at Mass is called the Nicene Creed and was drawn up by two Councils, one held in Nicea in 325, the other at Constantinople in 381. It was not, however incorporated in the Mass immediately. That came later when the Christians of Antioch decided that praying the Creed together at Mass would help them to resist any temptations to heresy and make them more aware of "the canons of our faith." Later the custom spread to Spain and into other European countries. Rome, however did not adopt it until after the eleventh century.

At Mass, then, the Creed is a kind of echo of what has gone before in the Gospel and homily and a sign post to what follows in the Eucharistic Prayer, the prayer of thanksgiving.

A prayer which unites

We should all try, then, whether we recite or sing the Creed to say it as a prayer which unites everyone in the Church. "Let the Creed resound," ordered a Council held at Toledo in 589, "so that the true faith may be declared in sound, and that the souls of believers, in accepting that faith, may be ready to partake, in communion, of the Body and Blood of Christ."

10.Prayer of the Faithful

GOD THE FATHER LIKES GIVING. Our Lord made this very clear when he told us that whatever we ask for in his name, the Father will give us. And yet many of us are very reluctant to ask him for what we *really* want and need.

Think again

One very understandable reason for this is that we are often a little afraid of praying before the Father like a spoiled child who never opens his mouth except to ask for things. But when our silence is due to a deep seated feeling that there is probably little God can do anyway, we really do need to think again. We are coldly ignoring Christ's promise when we pray with the implication, "I do not think you can do this, God."

The liturgy can help us a great deal here. Listening to the Readings and homily in the first part of the Mass is rather like going for a walk with God and letting him tell us about his ways. And there is one point he keeps emphasising. He is not an absentee landlord. Our God is bound up intimately with everyone and every thing in this world and his lordship is not as

Our intentions range from the concerns of the whole world to matters of local and personal interest.

limited as we are sometimes tempted to think.

Lord of All

This is why Prayers of Intercession, which we make after the Creed are a mixture of what one could call large and small prayers. Our intentions range from the concerns of the whole world to matters of local and personal interest. The Church *really* does believe that God is the Lord of All.

Ambitious prayers

Left to ourselves, we probably would not have either the concern or the faith and love to pray for the peace of the world and other enormous prayers like that. But when we make our Prayers of Intercession together at Mass we learn to make such hopes our own and to trust in the faith and love of each other. We are 'propped up', as it were, by the faith and love of the whole Church.

Smaller prayers

By the same token, the small prayers teach us how concerned God is even with the smallest details of life and this is why we should take these Prayers of Intercession seriously. Week by week they lead us, as an Eastern writer puts it, "to place the name of the Lord on every thing and every being on which our thoughts rest."

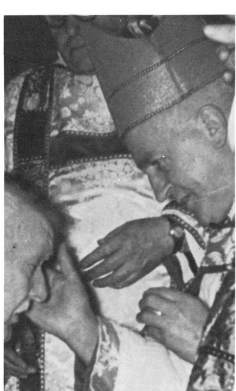

Left to ourselves, we probably would not have the faith and love to pray for the peace of the world . . . but when we make our Prayers of Intercession together at Mass we are 'propped up', as it were, by the faith and love of the whole Church.

11. The Two Tables

Priest and servers prepare the altar. As the scene changes from the lectern to the altar it is clear that a new stage of the Mass is about to begin.

AS SOON AS THE PRAYERS OF Intercession have finished a wave of activity sweeps through the assembly. There is a frantic search for the collection money; collectors take up the offerings. Priest and servers prepare the altar. As the scene changes from the lectern to the altar it is clear that a new stage of the Mass is about to begin.

"Two parts"

The Mass is divided into two principal stages — the Liturgy of the Word and the Liturgy of the Eucharist — which cannot be separated. In the "interval" between these stages we consider how "the two parts are so closely connected as to form one act

of worship." (*Introduction to Roman Missal*)

We receive Christ's word

We easily recognise that we are nourished and refreshed at "the table of the Lord's body". As we gather around the altar our communion binds us closer to Christ and to one another. But the altar is not the only "table". At Mass, we are seated, too, around "the table of God's Word." This is why in recent years the Church has instructed that "the treasures of the Bible are to be opened up more lavishly, so that richer fare may be provided for the faithful at the table of God's Word."

Before Christ gave his Body and Blood to the apostles at the Last

Supper he spoke movingly and instructively in words that transformed them. And in the Mass today the Word of God, the same Word who brought the world into existence and who saved us, continues to mould us into the Body of Christ.

We receive Christ's flesh

The Liturgy of the Word, then, is not a "time-filler" before we start the Liturgy of the Eucharist; nor is it a chance for a bit of Bible reading and a sermon which could as well be filled by saying our prayers. It is an essential part of the celebration of Mass. In the Liturgy of the World and the Liturgy of the Eucharist it is the same Christ we receive: the Word made flesh who transforms us into images of himself.

Ready to offer

The offertory procession continues the ancient custom going back to the second century when people brought bread and wine from their homes. The gifts, representing all that we have and are, are brought to the altar. But they are gifts now made worthy to be offered with Christ in the Mass. The Word of God has prepared and fashioned us to share fully in the great Act of Thanksgiving which is about to take place.

There is a frantic search for the collection money ; collectors take up the offerings.

The gifts, representing all that we have and are, are brought to the altar.

12. Preparation of the Gifts

THE FIRST CELEBRATION OF THE Eucharist was so simple. "As they were eating," we are told, "Jesus took some bread . . . then he took a cup."

Today, the taking of the bread and wine is surrounded with greater ceremony. The significance of that simple action is drawn out for us as we prepare ourselves for the high-point of our celebration. As we all share in the "preparation of the gifts" our minds and hearts are directed to praising and thanking God for them.

Developing ceremonial

In the first two centuries there was little ceremonial. Gradually the offertory procession and the prayers that accompanied the placing of the gifts on the altar developed. In the early middle ages, however, the offertory procession disappeared. The introduction of unleavened bread (bread made without yeast) meant that generally it came to be specially made and could no longer be baked in the kitchens of the faithful. The full force of the truth that *everyone* shares in what is to take place was weakened.

But the truth was by no means lost. The drop of water poured into the wine is traditionally understood to symbolise the faithful. And just as the water can no longer be separated from the wine, so our union with Christ through faith is so firm that nothing can separate it.

"My sacrifice and yours . . ."

The preparation of the gifts remains simply, then, the time when our gifts of bread and wine are offered to God, who is represented, as it were, by the priest and by the altar. At the Last Supper our Lord had to reach out and

"Jesus took some bread . . . then he took a cup."

The drop of water poured into the wine is traditionally understood to symbolise the faithful.

Quietly, the priest bows down in prayer.

The priest washes his hands, asking God to cleanse him of sin.

"take" the bread and wine. Today, at Mass, it is our duty and privilege to present them.

"May the Lord accept . . ."

And what a privilege ! As we present the gifts, which are now set apart for consecration, the awful reality suddenly confronts us. The partnership of God and man in creation is about to be continued in God's re-creation; in the coming of Christ. Quietly, the priest bows down in prayer, "not daring to raise his eyes to heaven" and then washes his hands, asking God to cleanse him from sin. Finally, priest and people together join in one concluding prayer that their gifts may be acceptable to God.

29

"Let us give thanks to the Lord our God.
It is right to give him thanks and praise.
Father, it is our duty and our salvation,
always and everywhere to give you thanks
through your beloved Son, Jesus Christ.
With love we celebrate his death.
With living faith we proclaim his resurrection.
With unwavering hope we await his return in glory.

Now, with the saints and all the angels
we praise you for ever:

Holy, holy, holy Lord, God of power and might,
heaven and earth are full of your glory.
    Hosanna in the highest.
Blessed is he who comes in the name of the Lord.
    Hosanna in the highest."

ET UNAM, SANCTAM, CATHOLIC-am et apostolicam Ecclesiam. The Latin words of the Creed are not so often heard now. And, perhaps, the pride that accompanied their singing is not so often voiced. But our hearts surely still swell as we proclaim our faith: "We believe in one holy catholic and apostolic Church." Our Church goes back to the apostles. We're proud of it! And, if it's the right kind of pride, we thank God for it!

Ours is the same faith as the apostles who followed Christ's life closely. And so our minds inevitably turn to their lives. As we assemble in the church on a Sunday most of us must wonder amidst all the other distractions, how did the apostles celebrate Mass?

The same celebration

It is an important question. For our faith is founded on the fact that our celebration of Mass is *exactly* that celebrated by the apostles. The apostles themselves recognised their duty to hand on *exactly* what the Lord commanded. When St. Paul described the Eucharist he was careful to emphasise that, "This is what I received from the Lord, and in turn passed on to you." (*1 Cor. 11:23*)

A variety of expression

We do not, of course, know the precise words that any of the apostles used in the Eucharistic Prayer, the high point of our celebration. If the words were written down at all they have long since been lost. Each apostle would have used different words, as did every bishop in the first three centuries of the Church's life; and this "variety" is reflected today in the four "Eucharistic Prayers" of the Roman Rite.

Our belief focuses on the Eucharistic Prayer. It is the central mystery of our faith; the core of our Christian life. It brings together all the elements which make up our faith. And so, although the words used have "varied" over the centuries, we can be certain that those elements have always been present. The Eucharistic Prayer today is the same as that used by the apostles.

Gratitude

In the next few pages we will briefly look at these elements. But, as we begin to look at the Prayer, we remind ourselves that it is, above all, a Prayer of praise and thanksgiving. The Prayer reflects, in other words, the central truth of our faith: that our Christian life is primarily a life of praise and gratitude to God.

The Eucharistic Prayer begins with the invitation to thank God and then gives the reasons for our gratitude. The earliest Eucharistic Prayer of which we have record goes back to 215 A.D. See how it begins:

"The Lord be with you.
And also with you.
Lift up your hearts.
We lift them up to the Lord.
Let us give thanks to the Lord our God.
It is right to give him thanks and praise.

We give you thanks, O God, through your dear child Jesus Christ, whom you sent us in these last days to save us, redeem us and inform us of your plan . . ."

These words, spoken 1750 years ago still survive, not simply in the deadness of an ancient parchment, but in the daily recounting of God's good deeds in the celebration of the Eucharist. The living tradition of our Faith continues in the Mass. We're proud of it! And we thank God for it! Let us give thanks to the Lord our God.

As we assemble in the church on a Sunday we wonder, how did the apostles celebrate Mass?

14. Eucharistic Prayer: Epiclesis

"Let your Spirit come upon these gifts to make them holy,
so that they may become for us
the body and blood of our Lord, Jesus Christ...

May all of us who share in the body and blood of Christ
be brought together in unity by the Holy Spirit."

IN OUR ATTEMPTS TO ENTER more deeply into the mystery of the Eucharist, we mustn't forget the part played by the Holy Spirit. Just before the narrative of the institution, or what is more commonly referred to as the consecration, the priest calls on the Father to send the Holy Spirit upon the gifts.

This apparently simple prayer enshrines within a few words an all-embracing cry from the whole Church. The plea of the priest is a plea which unites in one common desire those who stand around the altar in cathedral and concentration camp: "Let your Spirit come upon these gifts to make them holy, so that they may become for us the Body and Blood of our Lord Jesus Christ."

Calling on God

The prayer which calls on the Father to send the Holy Spirit has always been regarded in the Church as a very special and powerful one. In fact, such a prayer has even been given its own name, *epiclesis.* For anyone who understands Greek this word conjures up pictures of someone begging and invoking another for help. And this is exactly what we do in this prayer at Mass. We call from the depths of our hearts on God's name and invoke his power.

The Holy Spirit and Baptism

Saint Ambrose, writing in the fourth century, is at pains to remind us that in all the sacraments man can do nothing unless he begs and implores the assistance of divine power. It is not surprising, then, to learn that the earliest records we have speak of the use of the epiclesis, the prayer of invocation, at baptism. Actually, a little reflection on the sacrament of baptism can help us to understand the deeper significance of this prayer in the Mass.

Try and imagine it is a Sunday afternoon and, since you are passing the Church, you decide to call in and spend a few moments in prayer. On entering, however, you notice a little family group gathered around a baby. There is a baptism in progress. What would your reaction be to this situation? Would you stay and join in the ceremony or suddenly retrace your steps afraid of disturbing the intimacy of the occasion?

We are Christ's Body

If we feel outsiders at baptisms in our parish, then something is going badly wrong. None of us should feel constrained to slip out of the door quietly. As Fr. Louis Evely writes, "We who are baptised are brothers and sisters to a greater degree than if we had been born of the same mother and father. We not only belong to the same family but to the same Body."

Whenever we are at Mass, the memory of our baptism should never be far away. We can recall as we glance at the faces of stranger and friend that it is the Spirit, the first gift of Christ to his Church, who makes us into "one body, one Spirit in Christ". And, as the priest extends his hands over the offerings, we should remember that without invoking his power now we could never give true thanks and praise to the Father "through Christ our Lord".

As the priest extends his hands over the offerings he invokes the power of the Holy Spirit.

"On the night he was betrayed,
he took bread and gave you thanks and praise.
He broke the bread, gave it to his disciples, and said:
Take this, all of you, and eat it:
this is my body which will be given up for you."

"When supper was ended, he took the cup.
Again he gave you thanks and praise,
gave the cup to his disciples, and said:
Take this, all of you, and drink from it:
this is the cup of my blood,
the blood of the new and everlasting covenant.
It will be shed for you and for all men
so that sins may be forgiven.
Do this in memory of me."

Through the words of consecration the bread and wine on the altar are changed into the Body and Blood of Christ. The appearances of bread and wine remain. But the reality beneath those appearances changes. The reality is no longer bread and wine but Christ's Body and Blood. To describe this change the Church uses the word *transubstantiation.*

A belief challenged

Such a stupendous belief can never remain unchallenged for long. Not surprisingly, then, several little actions in this part of the Mass were originally introduced to emphasise some aspect of this belief which was under attack from heretics. This is the most likely explanation for the introduction of the elevation of the host and chalice in the thirteenth century.

A succession of attacks on the Real Presence sparked off among the faithful an intense desire to emphasise the belief. In French and English churches a custom arose of drawing a dark curtain behind the altar in order to make the white host stand out more clearly. The thurifer was warned not to let clouds of incense hide the altar from view. And, by the end of the thirteenth century, the large bell of the church was rung at both elevations so that those who were busy at home or at work in the fields might pause to praise the Lord.

The mystery of faith

It is impossible, of course, to fully enter into this part of the Mass simply by reading about its history. Here we are brought face to face with the *mysterium fidei,* the mystery of faith. "Lord, I do have faith," cried the father of the epileptic child, "Help the little faith I have!" Perhaps we all need to make his prayer our own.

"ON THE NIGHT HE WAS BETRAY-ed, he took bread and gave you thanks and praise . . . " In just a few brief sentences the priest, like a skilled master painter, sketches a vivid word-picture of the moment when Christ instituted the Eucharist. We call this word-picture the *narrative of institution* and, together with the words of consecration, it forms the heart and core of the Mass.

The words of consecration used by the priest are extremely ancient indeed. That is why they differ slightly from the words used in Scripture. Christians gathered to celebrate the Eucharist many years before the evangelists began the work of setting down the greatest story ever told. So we have in these words, beyond any doubt at all, a living link with the worship of the first men and women to follow in the footsteps of the Lord.

Although the priest actually speaks the words, at no other point in the Mass is his own personality more obscured. He does not say: "This is the body of Christ" but, emphasising our belief that Christ is at work among us, "This is my body." As St. Thomas Aquinas writes, "The priest bears the image of Christ, in whose person and power he utters the words of consecration."

16. Eucharistic Prayer: Memorial

"When we eat this bread and drink this cup,
we proclaim your death, Lord Jesus,
until you come in glory.
Father, we now celebrate this memorial of our redemption.
We recall Christ's death, his descent among the dead,
his resurrection, and his ascension to your right hand . . . ''

WE HAVE SEEN HOW THE CHRISTian community has always come together to celebrate the Eucharist. This "coming together" has been referred to over the years in many different ways: the Lord's Supper, Holy Communion, the breaking of the bread, the Eucharist, the Mass. The old Gaelic word for the Mass is *Aifreann,* a word which means "the redoing of the meal." This expression "the redoing of the meal", sums up all the other words. For when we come together for Mass we do so to repeat and recall what Christ did on the night before he died. That was the night he identified himself with the broken bread and the poured-out wine and in this way shared his life with those about him. And on that night he left us his command, "Do this in memory of me."

The passover meal

To understand what happened on that night we must go back to the Passover meal that Jesus celebrated with his disciples. The Passover feast was the greatest feast of the Jewish year. Every Jewish family gathered together to eat a special meal. This was no ordinary celebration: the Passover meal began with the question — "Why is this night different from all other nights?" In Jewish homes the answer has not changed since our Lord's time. "We were slaves to Pharaoh in Egypt, and would still be so, had not the Lord our God brought us out thence . . . ''

The Passover feast was, and still is, a celebration in memory of the happiest moment in the history of the Jewish People, their deliverance from slavery in Egypt. Everything on the table reminded the guests of the day God delivered the Chosen People from slavery.

The lamb: this was to remind them how the Angel of Death "passed over" those houses protected with the blood of the lamb.

The unleavened bread: this was to remind them of the haste with which they prepared their final meal in Egypt. The avoidance of leaven became a symbol of a completely new beginning.

The bitter herbs: the bitter taste reminded them of the bitter condition of the slave.

The Charosheth: this was a kind of paste made from fruit and nuts. This was to remind them how they had to make bricks from clay.

The cups of wine: there were four altogether and were drunk at different stages of the meal. These were to remind them of the four promises made by God. That He would deliver them from the Egyptians; that He would make them free men; that He would redeem them; that He would make them His People. (Exodus 6:6,7)

Once the table was set everything was ready. History was about to reach its climax. Jesus Christ was ready to celebrate the Passover with his disciples.

When the Passover meal was celebrated, the door of the room was always left open. Pointing to the open door, the guests repeated after the host "One day the Messiah will come to join us at our meal". It is tragic to realise that they did not accept him. "He came unto his own and his own received him not". (Jn. 1:11)

Jesus took bread and wine...

At every celebration of Mass we remember the feast of the Passover on Holy Thursday night. We remember how our Lord took the bread and wine and said over them "This is my Body, This is my Blood." Christ offers his life in sacrifice for the whole world.

Our Lord told us to repeat that meal and we do. To the casual observer the Mass is nothing more than a ceremonial recalling of an event long past. But to those who have been given the gift of faith, it is much more. It is a meal which actually brings those who eat it into full contact with the saving power of God.

This is the full force of the phrases we find in the Memorial Prayer which follow the consecrations:

Eucharistic Prayer I
"Father, we celebrate the *memory* of Christ, your Son."

Eucharistic Prayer II
"*In memory* of his death and resurrection..."

Eucharistic Prayer III
"Father, *calling to mind* the death your Son endured for our salvation..."

Eucharistic Prayer IV
"Father, we now celebrate this *memorial* of our redemption."

In each of these Memorial Prayers, the italicised words have a very specialised meaning. They are all ways of translating the Greek word *anamnesis*. And this is not a very easy word to translate.

Each time...

Words like memory refer in English to something or someone that is only mentally recalled. But when Christ used this word he used it to signify the actual making present of a past event. The Memorial Prayer remains so, then, that we are not simply recalling in a mental fashion the events of Christ's death and resurrection. "The mystical body, the Church," writes Father Wintz O.F.M., "can and does repeatedly link itself to the once-and-for-all sacrifice of Christ, just as St. Paul advised: 'each time we eat the bread and drink the cup we proclaim the death of the Lord till he comes'." (1 Cor. 11:26)

17. Eucharistic Prayer: Offering

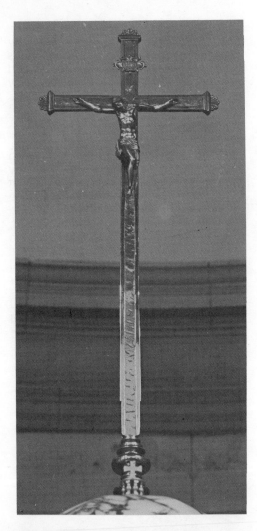

During Mass, either on the altar or near it, there is always the cross. It reminds us of that altar on which Christ chose to offer himself to the Father.

"WHY DID HE HAVE TO DIE?" The question is never far from our lips, whether it refers to the child killed in a road accident or the middle-aged executive struck down in the prime of life. The answer escapes us. It belongs to the realm of the "mysterious".

As Christians we find ourselves asking the same question of Christ's death on Calvary: "Why did he have to die?" The complete answer necessarily eludes us. It is part of the mystery of our faith: "Christ has died . . . Dying you destroyed our death".

The cross

Giving always takes something out of us; and in the ultimate giving of ourselves in death we are drained even of our blood. In life the cross is always near. And during Mass, either on the altar or near it, there is always the cross. It reminds us of that altar on which Christ chose to offer himself to the Father. On the cross, in the moment of supreme sacrifice, Jesus breathed his last with the words: "Father, into your hands I commit my spirit."

Christ has been raised

Into Jesus' lifeless body the Father poured his life-giving Spirit. The Son, who offered his life into the hands of the Father, now sits at the right hand of the Father, raised up as Lord.

The Mass is the same Sacrifice as that of Calvary. On our altar Christ is truly present. As the priest offers "in thanksgiving this holy and living sacrifice" he prays to the Father: "Look with favour on your Church's offering and see the Victim whose death has reconciled us to yourself."

The Mass and Calvary

There is a vital difference, however, between his offering on Calvary and the offering of himself which Christ makes at Mass. As Fr. John Schanz explains: "In the former case Christ was offering directly in his own Person; today he offers through the person of his priest and also in union with his followers, his Church. For the eucharistic sacrifice is truly the celebration of the whole Church, of Christ the risen head, of the priest in holy orders, and of the priestly people of God, the faithful, qualified by baptismal seal to share in the privilege of offering the family gift and eating the family meal." (*The Sacraments of Life and Worship*)

On Calvary, suspended between heaven and earth, Jesus was alone, isolated from the mankind which had rejected him. But, at Mass, we are united with Christ's offering. We are part of his Body, the Church.

One body, one spirit in Christ

It is as though the water which flowed from Christ's side at Calvary has washed us clean and enabled us to be one with him. At Baptism, of course, that is precisely what happened. But more! In the Eucharist we eat his flesh and drink his blood. We, who are nourished by Christ's body and blood, become one body, one spirit in Christ.

At Mass, in other words, Christ's offering becomes *our* offering: for we are Christ's Body. We are not spectators at the sacrifice of the Mass like the bored soldiers throwing dice; nor even like Mary and John looking up into the face of the dying Jesus. We *are* Christ. We are members of his

Body. We offer the sacrifice through, with and in Christ.

One with Christ in death and in life

As we more closely offer our lives with the offering of Christ's life on Calvary we penetrate more deeply into the mystery of death. As we learn to sacrifice ourselves with Christ we begin to realise why he died for us: "Unless a wheat grain falls on the ground and dies, it remains only a single grain; but if it dies, it yields a rich harvest." The realisation makes us cry out in a united acclamation: "Christ is risen . . . Christ will come again . . . Amen."

"We offer you in thanksgiving this holy and living sacrifice.
Look with favour on your Church's offering,
and see the Victim whose death has reconciled us to yourself.
Grant that we, who are nourished by his body and blood,
may be filled with his Holy Spirit,
and become one body, one spirit in Christ."

"Lord, remember those for whom we offer this sacrifice,
especially N. our Pope,
N. our bishop, and bishops and clergy everywhere.
Remember those who take part in this offering,
those here present and all your people,
and all who seek you with a sincere heart.
Remember those who have died in the peace of Christ
and all the dead whose faith is known to you alone.
Father, in your mercy grant also to us, your children,
to enter into our heavenly inheritance
in the company of the virgin Mary, the Mother of God,
and your apostles and saints.
Then, in your kingdom, freed from the corruption of sin and death,
we shall sing your glory with every creature through Christ our Lord,
through whom you give us everything that is good."

The prayer embraces the whole world... bishops... the departed ... Mary.

IMAGINE FOR A MOMENT YOU are in your parish church attending Mass along with your family and a few hundred other people. Now ask yourself two very searching questions. As you take part in the Mass, are you conscious that what you are doing is taking you far beyond the confines of your parish? Do you really take notice of the Eucharistic Prayers which are forever encouraging us to think big and unite ourselves to every living being and everyone who has gone before us in this world?

The prayers of intercession which follow the consecration certainly have this effect on a great many of us. As one writer puts it, "these are the prayers which keep nagging you to think bigger, to embrace the whole world: the Pope, the bishops, searching people everywhere; to draw in the past, the departed brothers and sisters of all centuries, including the first disciples."

The writer of the Letter to the Hebrews speaks of Christ as being Lord of time and space. "Jesus Christ," he writes, "is the same yesterday, today, and forever." And that is a thought well worth turning over in our minds a great deal when we are at Mass.

With Christ

Whenever we pray, "through Christ our Lord," we break, as it were, through the barriers of space and time. Christ is the *link* who unites past, present and future. When we join with him in giving thanks and praise to the Father, we do so along with millions of others. It is as if an invisible choir were crammed into our parish Church. Whether we are attending Mass in New York, Bristol, or Hong Kong, we are united to all those who have died, to all the living, and, indeed, we are given a foretaste of heaven itself.

With all men

It is our belief that around the altar is grouped the whole of humanity. And so, it is only natural that we try to remember them all. The fourth century fragments of the anaphora of St. Mark shows how the early Christians tried to do this in ever widening circles. "Give peace to the souls of the deceased, remember those for whom we keep a memorial this day, remember those whose names we know and do not know, guard our faithful fathers and bishops everywhere, and permit us to take a share in the lot of the holy prophets, apostles, and martyrs".

In the Mass we frequently refer to God as our Father. He is the creator of all things and all his creatures, living and dead are united through Christ in the same family.

What could be more natural, then, than to ask the Holy Spirit to bind us ever more closely together?

19. Eucharistic Prayer: Praise

"WHEN THE PRESIDENT HAS finished the prayers and thanksgiving, the whole crowd standing by cries out in agreement: 'Amen'. 'Amen' is a Hebrew word and means, 'So may it be'."

These words, written by St. Justin, describe how the heart of the Mass, the Eucharistic Prayer, was concluded about A.D. 150. At significant points of the Prayer — in the opening dialogue, after the Preface and after the words of consecration — the people have acclaimed their approval. They have offered the sacrifice with and through the priest. Now, with the "Amen" the people add their signature.

The words of the priest as he offers Christ's Body and Blood to his heavenly Father in what is traditionally called the "Little Elevation" crown all that has just taken place. Our minds and hearts are taken up, with Christ, into the life of the Trinity. We are drawn to praise God. Every true prayer ends in such a way. Our response can only be heartfelt and resounding: "Amen . . . So may it be."

**Through him,
with him,
in him,
in the unity of the Holy Spirit,
all glory and honour is yours,
almighty Father,
for ever and ever.
Amen.**

AT PRESENT THERE ARE FOUR Eucharistic Prayers in common use in the Roman Liturgy. (There are many more in Eastern Liturgies.) In addition there are Eucharistic Prayers for Masses with children and for Masses of Reconciliation: but these, of course, are not so widely used. Every Prayer contains the same essential elements that we have outlined. Now we briefly summarise the background to each of the four principal Eucharistic Prayers.

Eucharistic Prayer I

Known as the Roman Canon, this Prayer was the only one in use since the Roman Church moved from Greek to Latin in its Liturgy (about A.D.375). A few changes in the text have been made: among the most recent being the addition of St Joseph to the list of saints by Pope John XXIII in 1962. Over the centuries the most significant change was the growing tendency to say it silently so that it could not be heard by the people. Together with many other changes in the Liturgy this tendency was corrected in 1968.

Eucharistic Prayer II

This Prayer is based on the model given us by St Hippolytus, a bishop of the early Church, who has left us many valuable records of how the Liturgy was celebrated in about A.D. 215. The Prayer keeps the simplicity and brevity of Hippolytus' version although some changes have been made to bring it into line with the other Eucharistic Prayers. For example, the *Holy, holy holy Lord . . .*, probably a fourth century addition in the Roman Canon, has been added and the narrative of institution has been changed.

Eucharistic Prayer III

In the early centuries of the Church's life there were many Eucharistic Prayers in common use: although some of them began to omit those essential elements that we have been considering. The sobriety and clarity of Prayer I helped it to emerge successfully in competition against other Prayers. Prayer III, however, is made up from the storehouse of those very ancient texts which are most suitable but which passed out of use. Texts from Roman, Egyptian, Gallican and Mozarabic (Spanish) Liturgies are included. Thanksgiving is expressed primarily in the Preface, from which any of the eighty-one now in use is chosen.

Eucharistic Prayer IV

Prayer IV is founded on characteristics of Prayer of the Eastern Liturgies and is based on Scripture. Thanksgiving and praise are especially emphasised in the beautiful presentation of the history of salvation, which begins with the special Preface and includes the people's acclamation: *"Holy, holy, holy Lord . . . "* For this reason, no other Preface may be used with Prayer IV. Like all the Eucharistic Prayers, Prayer IV should be regarded primarily as a *prayer* and so it is valuable to meditate upon it at times other than at Mass.

20. Lord's Prayer

When we say the "Our Father" we are praying literally, with the words of Christ; and our hearts are being formed with the heart of Christ. In our minds we become the same as Christ Jesus.

CHRIST'S FIRST MENTION OF THE "bread of life" goes back to about 29 A.D., a year before he died, when, in the synagogue at Capernaum, he promised that, "anyone who eats this bread will live for ever." But the Mass takes us way beyond the year 29 A.D. It takes us into eternity.

The conclusion to the Eucharistic Prayer brings home to us that we are entering into the life of the Trinity. We pray through, with and in Christ, in union with the Holy Spirit: and we offer glory and honour to the Father, for ever and ever. The Mass unites us with Christ in the eternal offering of himself to the Father.

The proof of our union with Jesus takes place when we receive his body and blood. As the moment of communion approaches we remember Christ's words: "Anyone who eats my flesh and drinks my blood has eternal life . . . The words I have spoken to you are spirit and they are life." (*John 6:54.63*)

Christ's life-giving words

And so we recall, too, Christ's life-giving words spoken on a hill-top, less than ten miles from Capernaum, when he taught his followers how to pray: "Our Father, who art in heaven . . ." This is the model prayer for the Christian: it is the Lord's Prayer.

With one mind

When we say the "Our Father" we are praying literally, with the words of Christ; and our hearts are being formed with the heart of Christ. In our minds we become the same as Christ Jesus. So precious was this prayer in the early Church that it was guarded as a sacred mystery. It was never recited aloud or written down lest it be spoken by someone not baptised. Even those preparing for baptism were excluded from praying it.

The best preparation

In the first centuries of the Church's life communion simply formed the conclusion of the Eucharistic service and was not accompanied by special prayers. It was only natural, however, that the Lord's Prayer should come into use as the best preparation. As St Augustine wrote in A.D. 420: "The Our Father is like washing the face before going to the altar."

Our perfect prayer — in the words Christ taught us — helps us to approach the altar with greater confidence. The Eucharistic Prayer left us giving honour and glory to the Father: and so does the Lord's Prayer begin. It is as though the words we utter transport us into eternity. And so they do! For they are Christ's words.

Our sacrifice . . . our prayer

"Thy will be done on earth, as it is in heaven." Our attention, which has been centred directly on God in the first part of the Lord's Prayer, is brought, in this petition, to our own world of flesh and blood. Our sharing in the Body and Blood of Christ is a stark reminder of his sacrifice in which we also share. And so, in the words of the *Introduction to the Roman Missal,* "we pray for our daily food, which for Christians means also the eucharistic bread. And we pray for forgiveness from sin, so that what is holy may be given to those who are holy."

"Deliver us, Lord, from every evil . . ."

In the Middle Ages prayers for help in times of stress were inserted after the Lord's Prayer. Today, the priest simply expands the final petition and prays that "we may be kept free from sin and from all anxiety."

Our acclamation

Finally, as in all important parts of the Mass, everyone joins in an acclamation: "For the kingdom, the power, and the glory are yours, now and for ever." This ancient text is found in some of the early manuscripts of Matthew's Gospel as a conclusion to the Lord's Prayer. It was in common use in this country before the Reformation, although it was re-introduced in the Mass only comparatively recently. It is a final reminder that the Body and Blood of Christ are to give us eternal life: we are to be taken into eternity.

It is as though the words we utter transport us into eternity. And so they do! For they are Christ's words.

21. Rite of Peace

"The peace of the Lord be with you always."

his body and blood. We dare not approach the altar remembering that our neighbour has something against us. The greatest expression of our unity in Christ, of course, is our sharing in the body and blood of Christ. But it is desirable that this is expressed, too, in the ancient practice of exchanging a greeting of peace in some outward gesture.

What sign ?

It is as difficult today as it was in the medieval times to find a sign of peace that suits everyone. It may be more natural to follow a custom of the early Church by exchanging the sign at the beginning of Mass when we assemble; or, as was more common, to offer the sign of peace after the Readings. But although it is often hard to turn to our neighbour in greeting towards the end of the Mass, the teaching of Pope Innocent I in A.D. 416 is still helpful: "The people ought by means of the kiss of peace to make known their assent to all that has gone before."

A proof

We have just offered ourselves with Christ to his Father. We have celebrated the sacrifice to advance the peace and salvation of all the world. By our sign of peace we set the seal on our offering. We prove to God and to one another that we are prepared to work for the unity of all men in Christ.

EVEN IN MEDIEVAL TIMES THE sign of peace was sometimes a source of friction! The form of the sign varied according to the Rite and country. In some places it was an embrace; in others, each person would clasp the hands of his neighbour and kiss them; elsewhere, the people were satisfied with a mere bow. England, however, was different. It was the custom to keep on the altar during Mass a "pax-board" or "pax-brede", which was a small wooden or metal plate upon which was painted a figure of our Lord. This was passed from person to person before Communion, each one kissing it before passing it on to his neighbour. The trouble was that disputes arose as to the order of precedence in handling the pax-board!

A necessary part

Although this unedifying argument contradicted the very purpose of the Rite and led, in some measure, to its general disuse in the later Middle Ages, the sign of peace itself was always taken for granted as a necessary part of the Mass.

Peace and unity

The priest's prayer for peace reminds us that it was above all for peace and unity that Christ prayed on the night before he died and for which he gave

By our sign of peace we set the seal on our offering. We prove that we are prepared to work for unity.

22. Breaking of Bread

In the breaking of bread we recognise the presence of our Risen Lord . . . we recall the body of Christ being broken on the cross.

"This is the Lamb of God . . ."

AT THE LAST SUPPER OUR LORD took bread, *broke* it, and then gave it to his disciples. Today we still break the bread just as Christ did all those years ago.

The breaking of the bread takes place during the recitation or singing of the *Agnus Dei,* the Lamb of God. This invocation is called a confractorium, a "breaking song", and is all that remains of a much longer chant.

In the present rite of the Mass the priest continues the action of Christ by taking the large host into his hands and carefully breaking it into two parts over the paten. Then, after laying one of the two halves on the paten, he breaks off a small particle of the other and places it into the chalice.

In the earliest days of the Church, of course the practical reasons for this rite of breaking the bread were rather more obvious than they are today. One consecrated loaf was usually sufficient for the needs of most communities and the bishop simply broke it into as many pieces as were required. But the Church has always seen in these actions a deeper symbolic meaning which carries us even deeper into the mystery we are celebrating.

When the priest breaks the host in half we see represented in a symbolic way that moment when Christ broke the bread at the Last Supper. And like those two disciples on the road to Emmaus we recognise the presence of our Risen Lord in the very act of breaking bread. "Then they told their

48

When a priest drops a particle of the host in the chalice we are reminded of Christ returned to life in the resurrection.

story", records Luke, "and how they had recognised him in the breaking of the bread."

Christ's broken body

Spiritual writers have sometimes preferred a more mystical interpretation which saw in the breaking of the host the body of Christ being broken on the Cross. In fact, this interpretation can be traced as far back as the Council of Tours which in 567 in-structed priests to arrange the broken particles on the paten in the shape of a cross.

When the priest drops a particle of the host in the chalice we are reminded, in a rite which goes back to the fourth century, of Christ returned to life in the resurrection. His Body and Blood are united as a pledge of our own resurrection to new life.

All one in Christ

But here also we are reminded of an extremely ancient custom by which bishops in the early centuries expressed their unity in Christ with the priests and people of their diocese. Acolytes used to travel the various communities with particles of the host consecrated by the bishop. The priest would then drop the particles into his own chalice at this part of the Mass reminding everyone of the great belief we share. We are all one in Christ.

23. Communion

JESUS CHRIST COMMANDED US to come together to eat his body and drink his blood. And it is when we receive him in communion that the liturgy of the Mass reaches its completion.

In the present rite of the Mass the priest receives the body and blood of our Lord before communion is distributed to the congregation. He holds the host before each of those who are to receive and says, "The body of Christ". The response is quite simply "Amen".

One Body

This *Amen* should come to mean a great deal for each of us. It is our way of expressing our faith in the presence of Christ who binds us closely to one another and is the *only* way to the Father. "The blessing-cup that we bless is a communion with the blood of Christ", wrote St. Paul to the Corinthians, "and the bread that we break is a communion with the body of Christ. The fact that there is only one loaf means that, though there are many of us, we form a single body because we all have a share in this one loaf."

A voice from the fourth century confirms how this statement of faith in the unifying presence of Christ has always been at the centre of our Catholic life. We read in the *Mystagogic Catecheses* of Jerusalem: "When you approach, do not go stretching out your open hands or having your fingers spread out, but make the left hand into a throne for the right which shall receive the King, and then cup your open hand and take the body of Christ, reciting the *Amen*".

It is when we receive the body and blood of Christ in communion that the liturgy of the Eucharist reaches its completion.

Only when we receive him will we come to receive others into our lives as brothers and sisters in the Lord.

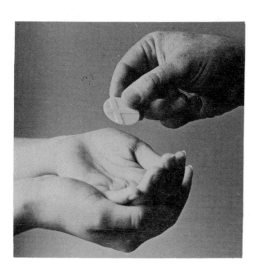

Up to the fourth century priest and people received communion at every Mass. But as Mass was usually only celebrated on a Sunday many people used to take some particles of the host home with them so that they could receive Christ each day before their main meal. A writer in the year 372 tells us that in Egypt "every lay person has the eucharist regularly in his home and takes it frequently."

Neglect

But in the fifth century there arose for the first time a rather sad practice which sadly seems to take root in the life of the Church from time to time. People began to stay away from communion. They had what they thought to be good reasons such as respect for the sacred species and awe and reverence for the divinity of Christ.

St. John Chrysostom was quick to point out that to stay away from communion was to ignore the command of Christ. "In vain and with sadness do we stand before the altar", he wrote, "for we find nobody to partake." His plea that we approach the Lord "full of trust that he will bind us into one family and forgive our sins" has been echoed by many since, particularly in our own times by Pope Pius X.

Receiving Christ

The mystery of the Eucharist is a great mystery indeed. But we must remember that we will only come to understand it if we approach Christ and receive him with faith into our lives. Only when we receive him will we come to receive others into our lives as brothers and sisters in the Lord.

24. Thanksgiving

"After communion the priest and people may spend some time in private prayer."

"IT IS THE MASS THAT MATTERS!"
It does not require a great deal of research to establish that this expression or some similar phrase has been a particular favourite of preachers in this country over the last four hundred years. Generation after generation has been brought up on the idea that the Mass is the centre of Catholic life.

The centre of our lives

"After communion", we read in the revised missal, "the priest and people may spend some time in private prayer." Perhaps this is a good time for each one of us to ask ourselves just what we mean when we say the Mass is right at the centre of our lives. After all, in a few moments when the priest has cleansed the altar vessels and said a final prayer he is going to ask us to "go in peace," and from now onwards "love and serve the Lord." And if our meeting with Christ, our sharing in the liturgy of the Mass, has no effect on our everyday lives then there is something sadly wrong in our spiritual thinking.

Giving thanks

The meaning of the Greek word *Eucharist* can provide us with plenty to think about in these moments of silence. It means *thanksgiving*. So perhaps we could profitably remind ourselves that when we say the Mass is the centre of our lives we are really telling everyone that thanksgiving and gratitude are the hallmarks of our daily living.

"The Christian," runs the old saying, "is someone who finds ninety-nine reasons to say thank you before he finds one to complain." That, in a nutshell, is an excellent description of one who lives the Mass.

As small children we became familiar with the phrase, "to be in a state of grace." It is helpful to notice that *grace* and *gratitude* are two very closely connected words. To be in a state of grace is in fact, to be a person of gratitude. It is to be the sort of person who, imitating the action of Christ in the Mass sees everyone and everything around him as gifts from the Father.

The one sure sign

In a world divided by selfishness, the Mass, the Eucharist, is the one sure sign of hope. Joined to Christ we can become unselfish and loving. As the priest puts away the paten and chalice for another day, we do well to recall that the sacrificial meal we have shared remains the one sure sign that peace in the family, peace in the community, peace in the world, will surely come.

In fact, one of the best things we can do is to make our own the prayer of St. Thomas which sums up so well the whole doctrine of the Eucharist: "O sacred banquet in which Christ is received, the memory of his passion is renewed, the soul is filled with grace, and the pledge of future glory is given us."

As the priest puts away the paten and chalice for another day, we do well to recall that the sacrificial meal we have shared remains the one sure sign that peace in the family, peace in the community, peace in the world, will surely come.

25. Concluding Rite

"Go, in the name of the Father and of the Son and of the Holy Spirit."

THE "BREAKING OF BREAD", THE "Lord's Supper", the "Memorial" is how the Scriptures described it. Today, different names are used: the "Eucharist", the "Holy Sacrifice", the "Mass". Whatever we prefer to call it we can only glimpse some of the many aspects of the celebration which, in the words of St. Thomas Aquinas, "contains the Church's entire spiritual wealth".

The Mass

In this country most Catholics refer to the "Mass". The word comes from the Latin, *missio*, which means *dismissal*. In words which are as ancient as the Latin Mass itself, the people were sent away with the command: "Ite, missa est"; which means, "Go, it is the dismissal". The people replied in the response that is still used: "Deo gratias" . . . "Thanks be to God".

How "missa" came to refer to the entire Eucharistic liturgy is not entirely clear. Possibly, the dismissal came to be closely identified with the final blessing, And then, in turn, the word began to be used for the heart of the liturgy when the principal blessing was made over the gifts of bread and wine just before the consecration. But whatever the explanation, the Latin word, "missa", that is, "dismissal", gave us our word, "Mass".

Christ's purpose

And it is a good word! It reminds us of Christ's very purpose in coming among us and within us. He is not a treasure to be received and carefully preserved — as a precious sculpture might be kept wrapped up in a museum. He is a treasure to be *shared*. And it is only in the dismissal that Christ's purpose of coming into the world to save *all* men can be fulfilled.

For while we remain in the church-building Christ's body remains like the dormant seed in the earth — or like that precious sculpture in the museum! It is only when we walk out of the church into our homes and places of work that Christ's body, into which we have been formed, begins to penetrate the world and to grow. At last, the Mass brings life to the world! And that is why Christ came into the world: that "we may have life and have it to the full". (*John 10:10*)

Go!

We cannot underestimate the importance of that command, "Go!" It echoes the last words of Christ on earth: "Go, therefore, make disciples of all nations; baptise them in the name of the Father and of the Son and of the Holy Spirit . . . and then, as he blessed them, he withdrew from them and was carried up to heaven."

To those who had known him and had eaten with him and had been formed by him that dismissal — that Missa — was not the end. It was the beginning.

It is only when we walk out of the church into our homes and places of work that Christ's Body, into which we have been formed, begins to penetrate the world and to grow.

26. The Presence Remains

From the earliest days the Church has reserved the Blessed Sacrament after the celebration of the eucharist. The sick and the suffering need the healing presence of Christ.

THE CATHOLIC CHURCH DOWN the years has always treasured the belief that the promises made us by the Lord have no time limit or built-in escape clauses. And we have only to look around us at Mass to see that trust and confidence in the Lord is a way of life for those who live in our parish. A notice at the church door tells us that Jane Smith and Peter Brown are soon to be married. What else but trust in God's faithful help can inspire them to commit themselves confidently to each other for a whole life-time?

If we look around our parishes we see a pattern of trust and confidence repeated over and over again. It is a pattern which repeats itself in the lives of the single, the married, priests and religious. We are all of us in the habit, even though we are sometimes hardly conscious of the fact, of living our lives on the quiet strength of the Lord.

Reservation

This universal need to lean on the arm of the Good Shepherd gave rise in the earliest days of the Church to the practice of reserving the Blessed Sacrament after the celebration of the eucharist. The sick and the suffering needed the healing presence of Christ.

We are all of us in the habit of living our lives on the quiet strength of the Lord.

But as time went on, the faithful began to see in this practice yet deeper aspects of the mystery. They began to see in the reservation of the Blessed Sacrament a sign, a reminder, that Christ's gift of himself in the eucharist has no time limit. As we kneel before the tabernacle, then, the message comes through to us in faith : "I have died for you ; I live for you and in you each moment of the day."

At the same time the tabernacle in our church is a reminder of the challenge that the Lord gives to all who share in the eucharistic mystery, "Love one another as I have loved you."

As we kneel before the tabernacle, then, the message comes through to us in faith : "I have died for you ; I live for you and in you each moment of the day."

27. "One Single Prayer"

IT IS AN OFTEN-REPEATED COM-plaint that the form of Sunday Mass varies from parish to parish: with the result, it is said, that "we never know where we are or what is going to happen next". Some Catholics are helped by such "variety"; some are confused; some are irritated.

The presence of Christ

In *The Mass in Pictures,* we have explained the different elements of the Mass, showing how they fit in with its general structure. Each element helps to build up Christ who, in the words of the *General Instruction of the Roman Missal,* is "really present in the assembly itself which is gathered in his name, in the person of the minister, in his word, and indeed substantially and unceasingly under the eucharistic species."

"Variety"

Some of these elements of the Mass are changeable. Some cannot change. Some must change. Some, as we have seen, have changed. As the Vatican Council reminded us, the "Liturgy is made up of unchangeable elements divinely instituted, and elements subject to change. The latter not only may but ought to be changed with the passing of time if features have by chance crept in which are less harmonious with the intimate nature of the liturgy, or if existing elements have grown less functional."

Principles of choice

The "variety" in the liturgy, then, is inspired by the Church. Many of the "variations" are at the choice of the priest. From among the alternative forms of celebration permitted by the law it is the minister's task to "choose in each instance those which seem most suited to the needs of the faithful and favourable to their full participa-tion." (*Instruction on the Worship of the Eucharistic Mystery, 1967*)

All share

The differences in the celebration of Mass reflect, in other words, the efforts of the Church and of her ministers to encourage everyone to share in the Mass as actively as possible. At times, of course, the individual needs and tastes of priest and people will con-flict! But such conflict is usually the result of forgetting firstly, that it is Christ who is present and leading us in the worship of his Father; and, secondly, that it is the task of *everyone* to share actively in that liturgy as fully and as clearly as possible.

One prayer to the Father

The priest's vestments are just one reminder that he is set apart to lead the community in the offering of sacrifice. He acts in the person of Christ in a special way. His task is to try and fulfil Pope Paul's prayer when he introduced the Roman Missal in 1969:

"Even if there is room in the new Missal for legitimate variations and adaptations we hope that it will be received by the faithful as a help and witness to the common unity of all. Thus, in the great diversity of langu-ages, one single prayer will rise as an acceptable offering to our Father in heaven, through our High Priest Jesus Christ, in the Holy Spirit."

Today's vestments are similar to the ordinary clothes worn by the laity in the Greco-Roman world. Over the amice (a scarf) is worn the alb, held by a cinture. The alb, a symbol of purity, is a survival of the ancient tunic or undergarment.

The chasuble, the outermost garment worn by the priest, was originally, like the everyday garment of Rome, a circular piece of cloth with a hole cut in the centre for the head. The shape has been altered over the centuries to allow greater freedom of movement.

28. The Mass in the World

"I AM GOD'S WHEAT; I AM ground by the teeth of the wild beasts that I may end as the pure wheat of Christ."

In these words of St Ignatius of Antioch we return to where we began *The Mass in Pictures.* We began with St Paul's description of the Eucharist written to the Corinthians about A.D.57 and St Justin's description of how it was celebrated just a century later in A.D.150. St Ignatius' famous words, addressed to the Christians of Rome where he was thrown to the lions at the public 'games', were written in the middle of that hundred years in 106.

The witness of St Ignatius vividly confronts us with the truth first taught by Jesus himself. When we eat the flesh of the Son of Man and drink his blood we are united with Christ even to sharing his divine life. We do not attend Mass as a spectator at some social spectacle, then, but as a sharer

Every good action of the Christian continues the celebration of the Mass. Every turn of the screw, every blow of the pick-axe, every chair dusted, every dinner cooked, every gesture, every word, every agony, every joy, becomes an offering to the Father which, because it is united with Christ's offering, is transformed.

in the Son's salvation. As St Augustine expressed it: "You have received that which you are; become that which you have received."

If you have entered into *The Mass in Pictures* as you enter into the celebration of every Mass your faith will have deepened. The Holy Spirit will have taken hold of you. What you have received in faith will have enabled you to become a new person. In the Mass we offer our human flesh to be ground by the teeth of sufferings — to be crucified — so that it may become the pure bread — the risen Body — of Christ.

A pretence?

If the Eucharist has failed to change us in the past is it, perhaps, because we try to use the Mass as an escape from the world? We enter the church and try to put aside our family sufferings and personal griefs. We pretend to be different to what we really are. And, at the end of Mass, we continue the pretence. We leave the church and re-enter the outside world only wishing that our life was different and that our sufferings would disappear. We misuse the church porch as a barrier between Christ and the world.

That is no celebration of the Eucharist! For when we come to Mass we come to offer our world of fallen flesh to God. We bring our sin, our suffering, our silly selfishness and offer these as Christ's body with Jesus himself as the head to our heavenly Father.

The world raised up

That offering of failure and weakness does not mean our suffering suddenly disappears. But it *is* transformed. It is given a new power: the power of Christ. And when we leave the church we bring his power to a fallen world in order that it may be taken over and raised up. The church porch becomes not a barrier between Christ and the world but a channel out of which God's Spirit can pour.

And so every good action of the Christian continues the celebration of the Mass. Every turn of the screw, every blow of the pick-axe, every chair dusted, every dinner cooked, every gesture, every word, every agony, every joy, becomes an offering to the Father which, because it is united with Christ's offering, is transformed. It is as though the earth and all that is in it is ground and kneaded and baked until our planet becomes transformed into a pure Host acceptable to God.

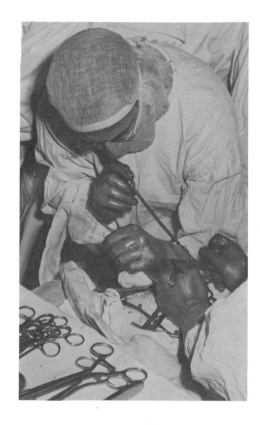

"I am God's wheat; I am ground by the teeth of the wild beasts that I may end as the pure wheat of Christ."

We will never feel the teeth of wild beasts; but we *do* experience the daily grind. Our bodies will never be broken in public exhibition; but our bodies *are* crushed in the privacy of domestic turmoil until they repose in death. That is our martyrdom: that is our Mass. May we celebrate it well.

# YOUR FAITH

Redemptorist Publications are pleased to offer this important publication written and produced by the priest-editors of THE MASS IN PICTURES.

If you have enjoyed this book, YOUR FAITH will prove the ideal follow-up for schools, for discussion groups and for individuals who wish to deepen their knowledge and understanding of Catholic teaching.

YOUR FAITH is divided into fifteen four-page sections — each section dealing with a different aspect of Catholic teaching. Points covered in the book include:

- Jesus is the centre of our faith
- Background to the life of Jesus
- Jesus revealed God to men
- Jesus is our redeemer
- Jesus sends the Holy Spirit
- The Church makes Jesus present today
- The New Testament
- The Mass
- The Sacraments
- Mary, Mother of all Christians

YOUR FAITH is an effective programme of Christian education which presents the fundamental truths of the Catholic faith in a simple and popular way. The enthusiastic reception of this book throughout the English-speaking world when it first appeared and the subsequent demand for its re-printing and translation into French indicates that it fulfils a real need in the Church at the present time.

Over 250,000 copies sold!
Two colours throughout: 64 pages
Only 75p/$1.95